AMAZING
Scriptures

A BOOK OF MORMON ADVENTURE OF COMICS AND MAZES!

BY NORMAN SHURTLIFF

CFI • An imprint of Cedar Fort, Inc.
Springville, Utah

AN ORIGINAL MAZE ADVENTURE BY
NORMAN SHURTLIFF

FLATTERS:	PLAY TESTERS:
JENNY SHURTLIFF	NEPHI SHURTLIFF
PATRICK SMITH	SCOTT WILTSE
ARLIN FEHR	

WWW.AMAZINGSCRIPTURES.COM

THE ADVENTURE CONTAINED HEREIN WAS BORN OUT OF A LOVE OF THE BOOK OF MORMON AND THE TALES IT TELLS OF GREAT HEROES, CUNNING VILLAINS, AND THE EPIC BATTLES BETWEEN THEM. I GREW UP WONDERING WHAT IT WOULD BE LIKE TO QUEST ALONGSIDE NEPHI, MORMON, AND MORONI. THIS BOOK IS A CULMINATION OF ALL THOSE IMAGINATIONS. THOUGH THIS BOOK IS INSPIRED BY AMAZING SCRIPTURES, IT IS ENTIRELY A WORK OF FICTION. TO FIND OUT WHAT REALLY HAPPENED, I URGE YOU TO READ THE TRUE ACCOUNT IN THE BOOK OF MORMON.
-NORMAN SHURTLIFF-

ISBN 13: 978-1-4621-2213-4

PUBLISHED BY CFI, AN IMPRINT OF CEDAR FORT, INC.
2373 W. 700 S., SPRINGVILLE, UT 84663
DISTRIBUTED BY CEDAR FORT, INC., WWW.CEDARFORT.COM

LIBRARY OF CONGRESS CONTROL NUMBER: 2018936986

COVER DESIGN BY NORMAN SHURTLIFF AND SHAWNDA T. CRAIG
COVER DESIGN © 2018 CEDAR FORT, INC.
LAYOUT BY NORMAN SHURTLIFF AND SHAWNDA T. CRAIG
EDITED BY KAITLIN BARWICK

PRINTED IN
THE UNITED STATES OF AMERICA

10 9 8 7 6 5 4 3 2 1

PRINTED ON ACID-FREE PAPER

AMAZING Scriptures

BOOK 1: THE MISSING MAP

LAMAN, LEMUEL, SAM, AND NEPHI HAVE
RETURNED TO JERUSALEM ON A QUEST TO
RETRIEVE THE BRASS PLATES OF LABAN.

AND IT CAME TO PATH...

HOW TO PLAY

(1) WHEN YOUR PATH IS BLOCKED

YOU CAN NOT MOVE THROUGH DOORS OR LOCKS
UNTIL YOU CAN UNLOCK THEM. COLLECT KEYS AND
ITEMS BY MOVING THROUGH THEM IN THE MAZE.
TAKE INVENTORY NOTES ON PG. IV.

KEYS UNLOCK DOORS   ITEMS OPEN LOCKS

(2) MOVING THROUGH THE ARTWORK

IRON RODS GUIDE YOU
THROUGH TUNNELS AND
UNDER OBSTACLES.

USE LADDERS, STEPS
AND OTHER OBJECTS TO
CLIMB TO NEW AREAS
OF THE MAZE.

(3) TURNING TO THE NEXT PAGE

ARROWS INDICATE WHEN IT'S TIME TO TURN
THE PAGE. FLIP TO THE PAGE NUMBER
SHOWN AND START AT THE ARROW OF THE
SAME COLOR.

LIAHONAS IDENTIFY
SHORTCUTS. FLIP TO THE
PAGE NUMBER SHOWN
AND START AT THE
ARROW OF THE SAME
COLOR AND LETTER.

(4) READING THE COMIC EVENTS

PAGE
NUMBER

EVENT
NUMBER

TURN TO A COMIC EVENT WHEN PASSING OVER ITS EVENT
TICKET IN THE MAZE. SOME ITEMS REQUIRE YOU TO READ
AN EVENT BEFORE COLLECTING THEM.

(5) WHEN YOU REACH A DEAD END

AT DEAD ENDS, *CAST LOTS* BY ROLLING A SIX-SIDED
DIE OR FLIP TO A RANDOM PAGE AND USE THE DICE
VALUE BELOW ITS PAGE NUMBER. COMPARE YOUR
ROLL TO THE TABLE AT THE BOTTOM OF THE PAGE.

MAKE A MARK IN THE HINDERED TALLY OF THE INVENTORY
ON PG. IV EACH TIME A DICE ROLL YIELDS A *HINDERED*
RESULT.

INVENTORY

BASIC ITEMS: THESE ITEMS MAY BE USED MORE THAN ONCE.

THIEF'S ERRAND	ROPE LADDER	WORK CLOTHES	SILVER VASE	MISSING MAP	SHOVEL

ADVANCED ITEMS: THESE ITEMS ARE ONLY USED ONCE. AFTER USE, REMOVE THEM FROM YOUR INVENTORY. YOU MAY CARRY AS MANY AS THERE ARE CHECK BOXES.

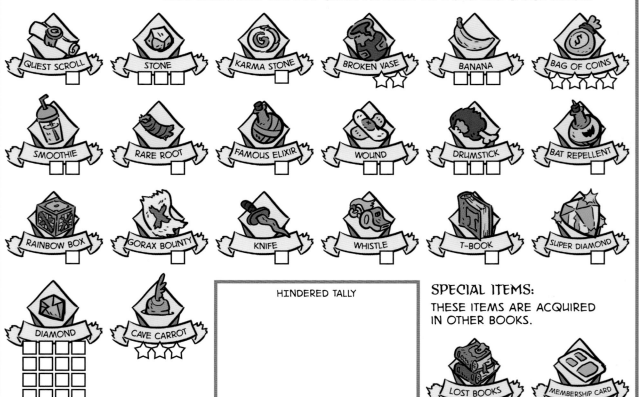

QUEST SCROLL • STONE • KARMA STONE • BROKEN VASE • BANANA • BAG OF COINS

SMOOTHIE • RARE ROOT • FAMOUS ELIXIR • WOUND • DRUMSTICK • BAT REPELLENT

RAINBOW BOX • GORAX BOUNTY • KNIFE • WHISTLE • T-BOOK • SUPER DIAMOND

DIAMOND • CAVE CARROT

HINDERED TALLY

SPECIAL ITEMS:
THESE ITEMS ARE ACQUIRED IN OTHER BOOKS.

LOST BOOKS • MEMBERSHIP CARD

IV

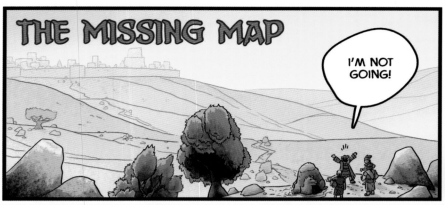

THE MISSING MAP

I'M NOT GOING!

I'M NOT GOING TO RISK MY REPUTATION FOR SOME BOOK!

BUT YOU'RE HIS APPRENTICE, LAMAN. YOU KNOW LABAN BETTER THAN ANY OF US.

HEY, WHY DON'T WE CAST LOTS?

WHENEVER YOU REACH A **DEAD END**, ROLL A DIE AND COMPARE IT TO THE CHART UNDER THE MAZE.

TALK TO LABAN

WHOEVER ROLLS A ONE WILL TALK TO LABAN.

FINE.

I DON'T BELIEVE IT!

FOLLOW ANY INSTRUCTIONS THAT POP UP!

GET

YEAH YEAH, "WHEN YOU **GET** AN ITEM, ADD IT TO YOUR CHARACTER SHEET. WHEN YOU **USE** AN ITEM, REMOVE IT."

I DON'T KNOW WHY OUR FATHER DEMANDS WE KEEP AN INVENTORY OF ALL OUR STUFF!

GO TO 2:2

YOU *COLLECT* ITEMS BY PASSING THROUGH THEM IN THE MAZE. SOME ITEMS MAY REQUIRE THAT YOU READ AN EVENT AS YOU APPROACH THEM.

TURN TO THE PAGE AND READ THE EVENT INDICATED BY THE *EVENT TICKET*. AFTER READING THE EVENT, ADD THE ITEM TO YOUR INVENTORY.

IF AN EVENT DOESN'T SAY WHERE TO TURN NEXT, JUST RETURN TO THE MAZE.

YOU'LL NOTICE THAT SOME ITEMS HAVE A *STAR* IN PLACE OF A CHECK BOX...

WHO ARE YOU TALKING TO? I'M OVER HERE!

...YOU CAN *FIND* THESE ITEMS IN THE SCENE AROUND THE MAZE.

OH LOOK, I FOUND A STONE. STOP TALKING CRAZY OR I *WILL* USE IT!

DON'T FORGET TO ADD THAT TO YOUR INVENTORY!

I DON'T NEED ANY MORE HELP! I CAN DO THIS ON MY OWN.

Grumble Grumble

DON'T FORGET TO CHOOSE THE RIGHT!

CHOOSE AN OPTION

THROW ROCK

3 : 5

OR

MURMUR

3 : 6

CAMPSITE

CAST LOTS AT DEAD ENDS BY ROLLING A SIX-SIDED DIE.

 LAMAN STUBBED HIS TOE.
HINDERED ONCE

 WANDERED OFF THE PATH
AND GOT LOST.
HINDERED ONCE

 GET

 GET

THE BACK WAY

CAST LOTS AT DEAD ENDS BY ROLLING A SIX-SIDED DIE.

 LAMAN STUMBLED INTO A POTHOLE.
HINDERED ONCE

 A SUDDEN DUST STORM MADE IT DIFFICULT TO SEE.
HINDERED ONCE

 PICKPOCKETED BY A THIEF, BUT ALL THEY GOT WAS A STONE.
*REMOVE 1 **STONE***

 WANDERED OFF AGAIN.
HINDERED ONCE

  NOTHING OUT HERE BUT SAND AND ROCK.

... AND THEN HIS *LIONS* ATTACKED ME!

I BARELY MADE IT OUT ALIVE.

I GUESS THAT'S IT THEN.

WAIT! WE CAN'T GIVE UP NOW!

WE CAN'T RETURN TO THE WILDERNESS WITHOUT GETTING THE PLATES! THEY ARE TOO IMPORTANT TO GIVE UP AFTER JUST ONE *LOUSY* TRY. WE MUST BE FAITHFUL IN KEEPING THE COMMANDMENTS OF THE LORD.

BEHOLD, OUR FATHER LEFT MANY PRECIOUS THINGS IN THE LAND OF OUR INHERITANCE. PERHAPS LABAN WOULD BE WILLING TO TRADE US FOR THE PLATES OF BRASS.

FINE. LET'S DO IT.

WHA!?

...

OLD CITY

CAST LOTS AT DEAD ENDS BY ROLLING A SIX-SIDED DIE.

YET AGAIN, LAMAN STUMBLED INTO A POTHOLE.
HINDERED ONCE

FELL INTO A PIT.
HINDERED ONCE

STEPPED ON A CRACK.
*GET 1 **WOUND***

STUMBLED OVER SOMETHING HE DIDN'T QUITE RECOGNIZE.
HINDERED ONCE

FELL INTO A PILE OF GARBAGE.
HINDERED ONCE

GET

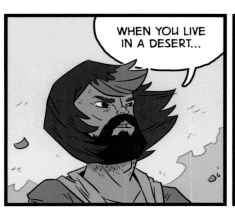

WHEN YOU LIVE IN A DESERT...

YOU GET USED TO THE DUST!

YOU'RE ASKING *TOO* MUCH!

YOU EXPECT ME TO GIVE THESE AWAY FOR *FREE?*

FINALLY AMONG *MY* KIND OF PEOPLE.

MARKET CHASE

CAST LOTS AT DEAD ENDS BY ROLLING A SIX-SIDED DIE.

BEHOLD A DANGEROUS BOUNTY HUNTER STALKS LAMAN! YOU MAY AVOID CASTING LOTS ONCE BY USING 1 *BANANA*.

AND INSTEAD

GO TO 11 : 14

BATTLE GORAX!

GO TO 15 : 18

A MERCHANT IS OPEN FOR BUSINESS.

USE 💰 ➡ GET 🛡

GO TO 11 : 15

HOW CAN I HELP YOU OFFICERS?

THE GUARD'S MAP HAS BEEN STOLEN.

WE WERE WONDERING IF ANYONE HAS TRIED PAWNING ONE OFF AT YOUR SHOP.

NO NO! MAPS DON'T INTEREST ME.

HEY!

WE'D STILL LIKE TO LOOK AROUND.

TAP! TAP!

BOO

AH!

HA HA HA! DID I SCARE YOU?

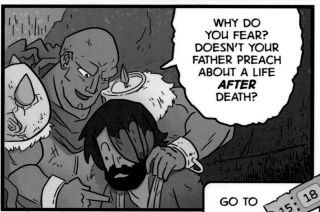

WHY DO YOU FEAR? DOESN'T YOUR FATHER PREACH ABOUT A LIFE *AFTER* DEATH?

14

GO TO 15 : 18

...AND NOW A GAME OF CHANCE.

I LIKE TO LET THE ROLL OF A DIE DETERMINE THE FATE OF MY ENEMIES.

IF YOU MANAGE TO ROLL HIGHER, I WILL LET YOU GO FREE.

HA HA! A FINE ROLL FOR ME!

NOW IT'S YOUR TURN.

WILL FATE SMILE UPON YOU? ANTICIPATION BRINGS SUCH EXCITEMENT.

REMEMBER, IF MY ROLL WAS HIGHER, I PUMMEL YOU INTO DUST.

GO TO 15 : 18

BATTLE GORAX

CAST LOTS BY ROLLING A SIX SIDED DICE.
YOU MAY INCREASE THE ROLL BY ONE FOR EACH OF THESE ITEMS YOU USE.

 YOU MAY AVOID BATTLE ONCE BY USING 1 **BANANA** AND INSTEAD GO TO 11 : 14

GET

HINDERED ONCE

LAMAN ESCAPES!

BATTLE LIONS

CAST LOTS BY ROLLING A SIX SIDED DICE.
YOU MAY INCREASE THE ROLL BY ONE FOR EACH OF THESE ITEMS YOU USE.

 YOU MAY AVOID BATTLE ONCE BY USING 1 **CAVE CARROT** AND INSTEAD GO TO 26 : 35

GET

HINDERED TWICE

HINDERED ONCE

LAMAN ESCAPES!

ENTRANCE

CAST LOTS AT DEAD ENDS BY ROLLING A SIX-SIDED DIE.

 LAMAN STOPPED TO ADMIRE THE FINE CARPETING.
HINDERED ONCE

 STOPPED TO TALK WITH AN OLD FRIEND.
HINDERED ONCE

 WHICH WAY IS IT AGAIN?
HINDERED ONCE

 MUST AVOID THE GUARDS!
HINDERED ONCE

 TRIPPED ON A FAULTY COBBLESTONE.
HINDERED ONCE

 A SERVANT GAVE BAD DIRECTIONS.
HINDERED ONCE

DINING HALL

CAST LOTS AT DEAD ENDS BY ROLLING A SIX-SIDED DIE.

A PESKY LION CUB SENSES THAT LAMAN IS UP TO NO GOOD. THAT, OR LAMAN HAS FOOD ON HIM.

WHEN CASTING LOTS, YOU MAY REMOVE 1 **DRUMSTICK** TO AVOID BEING HINDERED ONCE ON THIS PAGE.

   LAMAN IS TERRORIZED BY A LION CUB.
HINDERED ONCE

 GET

 LAMAN IS FIGURATIVELY TORN TO SHREDS.
HINDERED ONCE

 HID FROM THE LION CUB.
HINDERED ONCE

17

GET

I THOUGHT YOU SAID FATHER WOULD COME BACK TO HIS SENSES.

HE WILL.

YOU *KNOW* THIS IS ALL A WASTE, RIGHT, NEPHI? WHEN FATHER *DECIDES* TO MOVE BACK, HE'S GOING TO WONDER WHAT HAPPENED TO ALL HIS STUFF! AND *YOU'LL* BE THE ONE TO BLAME!

I'LL DO ANYTHING YOU WANT, LABAN. I JUST WANT TO BE FREE FROM MY FATHER'S FOOLISH WAYS.

RETURN TO THE DESERT, TO THE CAMP OF LEHI. MAKE SURE HE REMAINS HIDDEN THERE UNTIL I SEND WORD.

I HAVE A PLAN THAT WILL MAKE US BOTH VERY RICH MEN, BUT YOUR FATHER INTENDS TO THWART ME.

GET

HELP MY ARMIES CAPTURE LEHI AND I WILL SEE TO IT THAT YOU ARE HANDSOMELY REWARDED.

NO ONE WILL KNOW OF OUR LITTLE AGREEMENT.

MY ARMY WILL RALLY TO THE SOUND OF THIS WHISTLE.

GET

THAT'S RIGHT BOYS, I WORK HERE!

HE SEEMS AWFULLY PROUD TO BE A DISH WASHER.

SOMEONE'S GOTTA DO IT.

$

MY ELIXIR IS WORLD FAMOUS! I JUST NEED ONE *RARE ROOT* AND I COULD MAKE YOU A BATCH.

YOU MAY USE MY FAMOUS ELIXIR TO DECREASE YOUR HINDERED TALLY BY TEN!

IF YOU HAVE

YOU MAY ALSO GO TO

22 : 29

USE ➡ GET

UPPER CITY
CAST LOTS AT DEAD ENDS BY ROLLING A SIX-SIDED DIE.

 LAMAN FELL OFF A LEDGE.
HINDERED ONCE

 BONKED BY A FALLING STONE.
HINDERED ONCE

 FLIRTED WITH A SPENDTHRIFT.
HINDERED ONCE

 TRIPPED ON A LOOSE BRICK.
HINDERED ONCE

 HEARD SOMETHING SQUISH WHEN HE FELL.
REMOVE 1 BANANA

 SUDDENLY FORGOT WHERE HE WAS GOING.
HINDERED ONCE

21

31

THAT ROPE LADDER ACTUALLY WORKED OUT RATHER WELL.

32

I'M SORRY, BUT YOU CAN'T ENTER THE LIBRARY RIGHT NOW. YOUR *MEMBERSHIP CARD* HAS BEEN REVOKED.

COME BACK LATER WITH YOUR *OVERDUE BOOKS!*

HMM... I WONDER WHERE I PUT THOSE...

33

YOU THERE! YOU CAN'T START YOUR SHIFT WITHOUT A UNIFORM!

HERE, TAKE THIS ONE FOR TODAY.

GET

23

LIBRARY

CAST LOTS AT DEAD ENDS BY ROLLING A SIX-SIDED DIE.

 LAMAN WENT LEFT WHEN HE SHOULD HAVE WENT THE RIGHT WAY.
HINDERED ONCE

 HELPED A WOMAN CARRY HER BOOKS.
REMOVE 1 HINDER TALLY

 A GENEROUS PROSPECTOR OFFERS A TRADE:

FAULTY STREET TILE.
HINDERED ONCE

BASICALLY NOTHING HAPPENED.

USE ➡ GET

HA

HA HA

HA

HA

GET **2**

GO TO 15 : 19

HA! YOUR LIONS ARE NO MATCH FOR ME, LABAN.

NOW HAND OVER THE **PLATES OF BRASS!**

ONCE MY FATHER READS *THOSE PLATES* HE'LL COME TO HIS SENSES!

YOU'LL **NEVER** GET THAT BOOK!

GUARDS!

GET **2**

GORAX, FOLLOW HIM AND FIND OUT WHERE LEHI IS CAMPED. THEN ELIMINATE THEM ALL!

GET

36

YOU CAN'T GO IN THERE. ONLY *EMPLOYEES* BEYOND THIS POINT.

TURN BACK THE OTHER WAY BEFORE WE *ROUGH* YOU UP.

37

38

27

FAMILY ROOM

CAST LOTS AT DEAD ENDS BY ROLLING A SIX-SIDED DIE.

THERE'S NO PLACE LIKE HOME.
REMOVE 1 HINDER TALLY

DONE THIS A THOUSAND TIMES.
REMOVE 1 HINDER TALLY

LAMAN IS SUSPICIOUSLY COOPERATIVE.
REMOVE 1 HINDER TALLY

LOUNGING AROUND.
HINDERED ONCE

FOR THE MOMENT, THE COAST IS CLEAR. YOU MAY USE 1 *SMOOTHIE* TO REMOVE 5 HINDER TALLY MARKS. YOU MAY ALSO USE 1 *FAMOUS ELIXIR* TO REMOVE 10 HINDER TALLY MARKS.

28

GARDENS

CAST LOTS AT DEAD ENDS BY ROLLING A SIX-SIDED DIE.

 A HUNGRY BIRD SWOOPED DOWN FOR A SNACK.
*REMOVE 1 **BANANA***

 NEPHI TIDIED UP THE PLACE.
HINDERED ONCE

 ATE SOME YUMMY FRUIT.
*REMOVE 1 **WOUND***

 WHACKED BY A BRANCH.
HINDERED ONCE

 LEMUEL TOOK A NAP.
HINDERED ONCE

 BASKED IN THE SUNLIGHT.
*REMOVE 1 **WOUND***

29

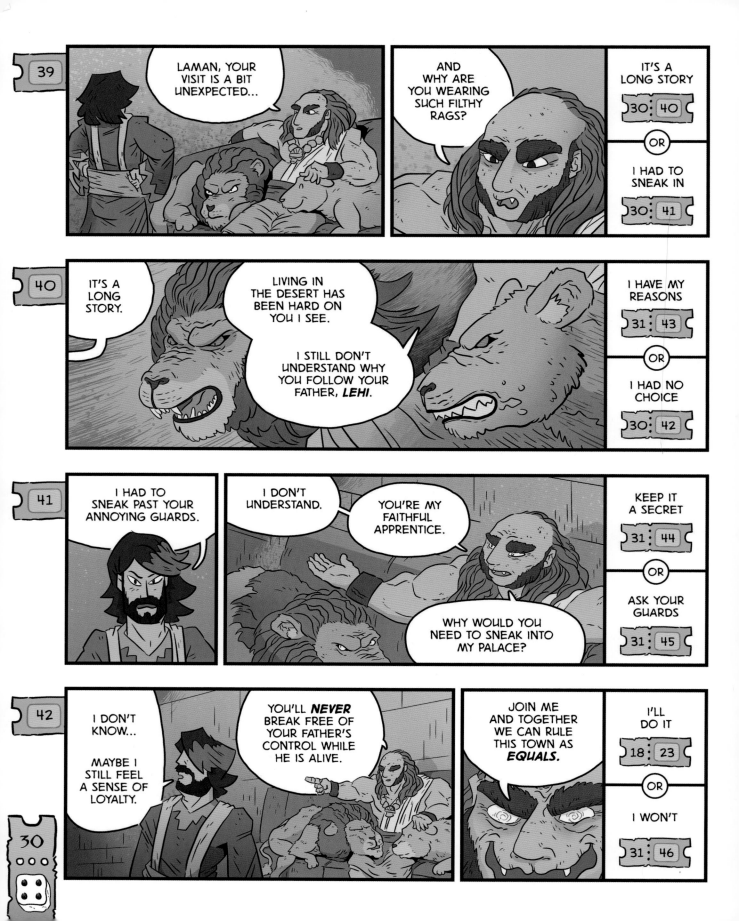

43

IN ORDER TO MAINTAIN MY BIRTHRIGHT, I **MUST** OBEY MY FATHER.

WHAT IF I TOLD YOU THAT I COULD MAKE YOU FAR RICHER THAN YOUR INHERITANCE WOULD?

BUT **FIRST**, YOUR FATHER WOULD NEED TO BE PUT ON TRIAL FOR HIS CRIMES.

I'LL DO IT
18 : 23

OR

I WON'T
31 : 46

44

I CAN'T HAVE ANYONE KNOW THAT I'M ON MY FATHER'S ERRAND!

YOUR FATHER HAS MADE AN ENEMY OF HIMSELF IN THIS TOWN.

MY FATHER IS A FOOL!

DO ME A FAVOR AND I **WILL** SEE THAT YOU TAKE HIS PLACE ON THE COUNCIL.

ANYTHING FOR YOU
18 : 22

OR

I DON'T KNOW
30 : 42

45

YOUR GUARDS WOULDN'T LET ME IN!

BECAUSE YOUR FATHER HAS CAUSED ME A GREAT DEAL OF TROUBLE.

HOW DO I KNOW LEHI HASN'T SENT YOU HERE TO CAUSE EVEN MORE?

I'LL DO ANYTHING
18 : 22

OR

I CAME FOR THE PLATES
35 : 48

46

WHAT!? I CAN'T BETRAY MY OWN FATHER!

LOOK, LABAN, I **ONLY** CAME HERE FOR THE PLATES OF BRASS.

HOW DO **YOU** KNOW OF THE BRASS PLATES?

ARE YOU THE THIEF THAT STOLE MY **MAP?**

YOU'LL WISH YOU NEVER CROSSED ME, LAMAN!

31

GO TO 26 : 34

THE HOUSE OF LABAN

CAST LOTS AT DEAD ENDS BY ROLLING A SIX-SIDED DIE.

IF YOU'VE MADE IT THIS FAR WITH A HINDERED TALLY OF LESS THAN TEN, LAMAN ARRIVES IN TIME TO OVERHEAR A SECRET CONVERSATION AS THE PLOT THICKENS.

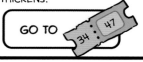

GO TO 34 : 47

NARROWLY ESCAPED HARM!

THAT PESKY LION CUB RANG THE ALARM!

GO TO 26 : 34

THE LION CUB WON'T LET GO. *HINDERED ONCE.*

LAMAN IS LITERALLY TORN TO SHREDS. *GET 1 **WOUND***

FAVORITE SPOT

CAST LOTS AT DEAD ENDS BY ROLLING A SIX-SIDED DIE.

 LEMUEL LIKES TO LOITER.

 STILL CONFUSED BY THEES AND THOUS.
HINDERED ONCE

 NEARLY FINISHED BUT STILL TIME FOR ONE MORE DEAD END.
HINDERED ONCE

 TOOK A BREATHER BEFORE RETURNING TO HIS BROTHERS.
HINDERED ONCE

 PONDERED HIS NEXT MOVE.
HINDERED ONCE

 AFTER THE END COMES THE BEGINNING.

33

I'M NOT HERE TO CAUSE ANY TROUBLE. I'VE JUST COME TO BORROW THE PLATES OF BRASS.

YOU **SNEAK** PAST MY GUARDS AND COME UNANNOUNCED.

LEHI HAS SURELY SENT YOU TO STEAL THE BRASS PLATES! HASN'T HE?

YOU SHOULD **NEVER** HAVE RETURNED!

GO TO 26 : 34

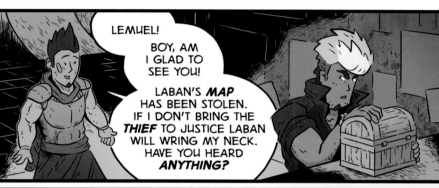

LEMUEL! BOY, AM I GLAD TO SEE YOU! LABAN'S **MAP** HAS BEEN STOLEN. IF I DON'T BRING THE **THIEF** TO JUSTICE LABAN WILL WRING MY NECK. HAVE YOU HEARD **ANYTHING?**

NO.

WELL, IF YOU DO HEAR ANYTHING YOU'VE **GOT** TO LET ME KNOW.

IT'S GOOD TO HAVE YOU BACK, LEMUEL!

I WILL.

CLICK

GET

THE CAVE 1

CAST LOTS AT DEAD ENDS BY ROLLING A SIX-SIDED DIE.

GET 💎

SAM GETS A LITTLE TOO
CLOSE TO THE EDGE.

FALSE ALARM!

SAM TRIPS!
HINDERED ONCE

SAM FALLS IN A HOLE.
HINDERED ONCE

Sam AND THE Secret Mine

THE CAVE II

CAST LOTS AT DEAD ENDS BY ROLLING A SIX-SIDED DIE.

  GET

 SAM FALLS THROUGH A HOLE IN THE FLOOR.

42C

 SAM DROPS A DIAMOND DOWN A HOLE.
REMOVE 1 DIAMOND

THE SECRET MINE

CAST LOTS AT DEAD ENDS BY ROLLING A SIX-SIDED DIE.

IF YOU HAVE YOU MAY IGNORE ANY ODD-NUMBERED ROLLS.

 A SWARM OF BATS! *HINDERED TWICE*

 A BAT STEALS A DIAMOND. *REMOVE 1* **DIAMOND**

 BATS, WHY DID IT HAVE TO BE BATS? *HINDERED ONCE AND REMOVE* **1 DIAMOND**

  GET

 SAM TRIPS AGAIN! *HINDERED ONCE*

   GET

THE DARK PIT

CAST LOTS AT DEAD ENDS BY ROLLING A SIX-SIDED DIE.

 IT'S GETTING REALLY DARK IN HERE...

 EEK! SOMETHING BRUSHED UP AGAINST SAM'S LEG...

SAM GETS LOST IN THE DARK.
HINDERED ONCE

 A BAT PESTERS SAM.
HINDERED ONCE

IT WAS PROBABLY NOTHING.

 SAM SINGS A HYMN TO CALM HIS NERVES.
REMOVE 3 HINDER TALLY MARKS.

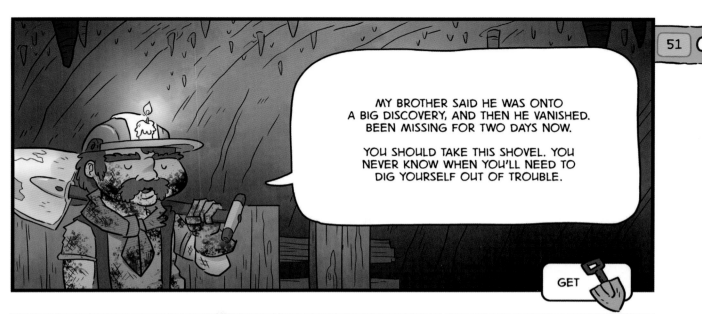

MY BROTHER SAID HE WAS ONTO A BIG DISCOVERY, AND THEN HE VANISHED. BEEN MISSING FOR TWO DAYS NOW.

YOU SHOULD TAKE THIS SHOVEL. YOU NEVER KNOW WHEN YOU'LL NEED TO DIG YOURSELF OUT OF TROUBLE.

GET

THANK YOU FOR SAVING ME, YOUNG MAN.

WITHOUT MY *SHOVEL* I DIDN'T KNOW HOW I WAS GOING TO DIG MYSELF OUT OF HERE.

TAKE THIS DIAMOND AS A GIFT.

GEE, THANKS!

GET

43

MAP OF JERUSALEM

HOUSE OF LABAN

(32)
(17) DINING HALL
(16) ENTRANCE
(24) LIBRARY
(20) UPPER CITY
(33) FAVORITE SPOT
(28) FAMILY ROOM
(29) GARDENS
(9) OLD CITY
(13) MARKET CHASE
(6) BACK WAY
(4) CAMPSITE
(36) THE CAVE

CONGRATULATIONS!

YOU'VE REACHED THE END OF THIS MAZE ADVENTURE. NOW IT'S TIME TO SEE HOW WELL YOU DID. YOU MAY REDUCE YOUR HINDERED TALLY ONCE FOR EACH OF THESE ITEMS YOU HAVE REMAINING IN YOUR INVENTORY. THEN COMPARE YOUR SCORE TO THE CHART BELOW.

HINDERED TALLY

1-10	NEPHI ALWAYS WINS
11-20	SAM DOES ALL RIGHT
21-30	LEMUEL, MEH
31-40	LAMAN TRIES AGAIN

THE EVER-EXPANDING MAZE

THERE ARE MANY MORE MAZES TO COME, AND EACH CONNECTS TO CREATE A GRAND WORLD OF MAZES. LOOK FOR THE GOLDEN PLATES SYMBOL THROUGHOUT THE SERIES. THEY IDENTIFY THE CONNECTING ROUTES BETWEEN EACH BOOK.

YOU CAN ALSO CARRY SPECIAL ITEMS BETWEEN ADVENTURES TO UNLOCK SPECIAL EVENTS AND MORE AMAZING EQUIPMENT. ANY UNUSED ITEMS IN THIS ADVENTURE WILL LIKELY BE USED IN A FUTURE MAZE.

THE ADVENTURE CONTINUES!